THE PRESENCE OF NOISE

A TEACHER'S HEART

JUDY ROBERTS

WESTBOW
PRESS®
A DIVISION OF THOMAS NELSON
& ZONDERVAN

WestBow Press books may be ordered through booksellers or by contacting:

WestBow Press
A Division of Thomas Nelson & Zondervan
1663 Liberty Drive
Bloomington, IN 47403
www.westbowpress.com
844-714-3454

Scripture taken from the King James Version of the Bible.

ISBN: 978-1-6642-2462-9 (sc)
ISBN: 978-1-6642-2461-2 (e)

Print information available on the last page.

WestBow Press rev. date: 03/12/2021

DEDICATION:

To Tommy, Tony and Tom

John 14:6
saith unto him, I am the way, the truth, and the
life: No man cometh unto the Father, but by Me.

Book cover by Ashley Roberts

CONTENTS

CONTENTS

1

AN AWAKENING

> But the fruit of the Spirit is love,
> joy, peace, longsuffering, gentle-
> ness, goodness, faith, meekness, tem-
> perance: against such there is no law.
> Galatians 5:22-23

As I set out on this journey of retirement, I knew that I had to exercise to get my blood pressure down and hopefully lose a few pounds in the process. Walking was my solution! I just didn't realize what an awesome solution it was! As I strolled through my beautiful tree-laden yard, God would open the recesses of my mind to the treasures that I thought were hidden so deep, to never emerge again. As I walked, God reached deep into this teacher's soul and helped me to remember the teacher that I was once honored to be! As my mind relaxed, God uncovered precious memories that I began to record. He showed me how to weave these stories with the poetry that was still contained in the two notebooks that I treasured. I'm so excited to share these words, feelings and thoughts that God has placed in this teacher's heart. Walk with me down memory lane and I will share my heart with you.

> Ointment and perfume rejoice
> the heart; so doth the sweetness
> of a man's friend by hearty counsel.
> Proverbs 27:9

My precious friend that taught next door to me, would communicate with me through notes brought by one of her students. Cell phones weren't allowed in the classroom back then! One day she sent a note with these instructions, "We are going to start on a Master's Degree and get a flu shot". I'm a follower of those I admire or maybe I trusted this friend with my whole heart, so we went to the MS Health Department and got both a flu and pneumonia shot. Later that week we started the process to register for Masters of Elementary Education classes. One of these classes had a profound effect on my classroom. Co-Operative Learning taught by a professor from William Carey College spoke to my heart! In her class I learned that children don't have to be in straight lines or be quiet to learn. This was an epiphany for me! I incorporated all I was learning into my classroom and the change was pure magic! The children were learning from each other as well as from me. They were learning to think, process information and have fun at the same time. And most surprising of all, this overly structured teacher was actually enjoying teaching again. I searched for ways to incorporate grouping within my structured setting. Writing group poetry as a way to review important facts across the curriculum evolved. I knew that most children processed and remembered information by placing that information into a different genre. I, also, knew that children love rhythm and rhyme. Rhyming words are the building blocks of learning to read and to spell. So I combined cooperative grouping, reviewing and processing information and poetry into a strategy that was enjoyed by the children and by me! So began the year of my metamorphosis!

Both of my principals knew that I felt most productive and comfortable in a quiet classroom with the desks and children in straight rows. They were surprised to peek inside my classroom and see desks in groups, talking among the students and me enjoying the controlled discussions. Every Friday the sign would appear on my door, "The Absence of Noise is not the Presence of Learning." The children would be in groups and 100% of the children would be engaged in the learning process. I knew that my attitude toward cooperative learning activities was the biggest indicator of success or failure. My professor even requested that I video my classroom during one of our poetry lessons! She used the video in her classes to show that cooperative learning is possible in the lower grades. I still remember that day! The children did an excellent job remembering their duties within their group and the resulting video was awesome! This request truly encouraged my efforts to include cooperative learning each day. During those days, I was never more proud of my students or more tired at the end of the day!

2

THE FRUIT OF LOVE

And now abideth faith, hope, charity, these three; but the greatest of these is charity. 1 Corinthians 13:13

I learned early on to listen to my students. One morning a student came to my desk and shared that his mama's rings might be down the bathroom sink drain. I casually replied," OK, thank you," and went straight and called his mom. She had been looking for her rings all morning. She immediately called a plumber and guess what! Her rings were in the drain just like her sweet and slightly guilty son had told me. The plumber told her that if anyone had run the water, the wedding rings would have been gone forever! Another crisis averted just by listening to a tiny voice at the busiest time of the morning!

Another busy morning produced the sweetest compliment ever! A precious young student came to my desk with a question about the morning assignment. She began with her question and then paused and whispered, "You smell so good!" I sincerely thanked her as I tried to recall the name of the perfume that I had used that morning and then she proceeded to say, "You smell just like my grandma!" At the time, I didn't realize the comment was a compliment, but I do now. It was the best compliment ever!

I learned to always investigate noisy children gathered in a group. One morning I noticed one of my students proudly showing off a hundred dollar bill. I quickly confiscated the money and called his mom. She had told her child to get a dollar from her billfold for a treat at recess and he had mistakenly gotten the wrong bill. She was so appreciative! It was her grocery money! Another morning during rush to get the children seated for the day, I noticed a student giving coins away. As I looked closer, I could see that these coins were not the normal nickels and dimes that most children have. This child had brought his grandfather's coin collection to school and was giving all the coins to his friends. I collected all the coins that were held by my students and called his mom. She knew immediately what had happened. We never recovered all the coins because he gave some away on the bus that morning.

One afternoon my class and another class were having music class together. They were meeting that day in Mrs. McMichael's classroom and I was busy in my classroom during these few minutes of free time. The music teacher sent two of my students to get me because several of my children were not behaving. I stalked up that hall aggravated to no end! Wow, was I in shock when I walked into a surprise birthday party for me! Birthday Cake and Humble Pie were a delicious ending to that day!

Another day as I was leading the class in our morning activities, I noticed two little divas on the front row giggling and pointing at my feet. As

I looked down, I couldn't believe I had on a black shoe and a brown shoe! I gave everyone from the office staff to the cafeteria workers, and especially the children a good laugh that day! The noise of laughing children always makes my heart smile and I learned to laugh with them.

The most meaningful comment ever said to me happened one day close to Christmas. One of my little girls related to me something that touched my heart deeply. This little girl was living in one of the hardest situations I've ever witnessed. She was an only child, her mother had cancer and wasn't expected to live through Christmas. She told me that I was the fairest teacher in the whole world. She said that I didn't have favorites and that I loved everyone the same. What an observation by a child! I pray that I never had favorites and that I did love each child the same. I heard a woman once speak on television about her many children. If I remember correctly, she had twelve. The reporter asked her if she loved one of them the most. She replied, "I love the one most that needs the most love that day. I listen to my children, search their eyes and their hearts, see their needs and love that one the most that day." As a teacher, I can only hope and pray that I loved the one that needed the most love each and every day.

Each spring my class and I raised butterflies. The Butterfly Garden came with a home for the butterflies and a coupon for caterpillars. The children fed the caterpillars and watched amazed as each one crawled upon a limb and began to transform into a chrysalis. The children counted the days till the metamorphosis would be complete and a beautiful butterfly would emerge from each cocoon. The children fed the newly hatched butterflies on sugar water soaked in paper towels. As the weather became warmer, it was safe to let the butterflies gain their freedom. We had a picnic lunch for the children on that day and many parents appeared to be with their child as we said goodbye to our charges. Not a dry eye was to be seen that day as I unzipped the top of the Butterfly Garden. As the butterflies were lifted on the soft breeze, there were shrieks of delight that hung on the butterflies like tails on a kite. As I think of the emotions of this day, I'm reminded of the last day of school each year as I hugged and kissed each little one goodbye. I had been their teacher, friend, protector and biggest fan for a whole year. As I watched through teary eyes, I knew they were taking part of my heart with them that last noisy day. As I glanced toward the sidewalk, there stood more teachers amid the noise with the same teary smile and I knew God gives special hearts to teachers: always big enough to love one more child, hearts that love each child as their own and hearts that have to say goodbye every May. To have a teacher's heart is a priceless treasure!

Freedom

By Judy Roberts

Butterfly, butterfly lifted on the gentle breeze,
Floating in and out of the clouds with ease.
Where will you fly, our fluttering friend?
Enjoy your freedom and playground without end!
An egg, a caterpillar, a chrysalis, then an adult,
Metamorphosis is amazing; a butterfly, the result!
The days hidden away were so carefully spent,
Like a colorful clown with your own special tent.
Your anticipated appearance was a magical treat.
We waited and wished and wiggled in our seat!
Each morning we rushed inside,
our charges to see,
And dreaded the day we must set you free!
Spread your wings, our friend,
and fly far, far away,
But please promise to return and visit one day.
One unexpected morn we'll hear
the flutter of tiny wings,
And the melody of our joyful
hearts will silently sing!

The Holy Spirit sent this poem to me after I had gone to bed early one night with a migraine. As I was lying there waiting for the medicine to work and thinking about my first glimpse that day of the beautiful butterfly you see on the cover, words kept flowing through my mind until I finally got up and found a pencil and paper. I'm always amazed at what God will do when I open my mind and heart to His words. I'm so thankful to be this broken vessel and for opportunities for His words to flow through me!

3

THE FRUIT OF JOY

✣ Thou wilt show me the path of life:
   in thy presence is fullness of joy; at
thy right hand there are pleasures for
evermore. Psalm 16:11

"Lord, I'm so excited about writing today!" This was my thought as I wrote what the Lord laid on my heart during my morning walk. I'm always excited to open my heart and my mind, but today was extra special. His message to me was about the freedom I experienced in my classroom which many teachers don't have today. It has been a true blessing to always work for principals that encourage morning devotionals, reciting the pledge and in some schools letting the children lead in the Lord's Prayer. In twenty-nine years I only had one parent disagree because I wouldn't read from his version of a Bible story book. He eventually agreed to let his child stay in the classroom during our morning devotional which consisted of a story from a King James Version Bible storybook and the Pledge. I stood for what God had laid on my heart, and He blessed my efforts with His Joy! As I finished the Old Testament Bible stories one year, I asked the children what they thought the main idea of these stories might be. Finding the main idea of a story in third grade is a huge skill. I was amazed at their level of perception! They agreed that the people were jealous of each other. That afternoon I glanced back over each story and sure enough someone in each story was jealous and the jealousy created sin in their lives. Out of the minds of my babies! They were so right!

I also read to my class each day after recess. They needed a time to refocus and a few minutes to rest and I loved sharing my favorites with them. The list of books over the years changed, but there were a few that were a constant in my classroom. I have listed these favorites of mine below with the author:

The Courage of Sarah Noble	Alice Dalgliesh
Sarah, Plain and Tall	Patricia MacLachlan
Skylark	Patricia MacLachlan
The Lion, the Witch, and the Wardrobe	C.S. Lewis
A Series of Unfortunate Events	Lemony Snicket
The Whipping Boy	Sid Fleischman
The Secret Garden	Frances Hodgson Burnett
James and the Giant Peach	Roald Dahl
Charlie and the Chocolate Factory	Roald Dahl
Where the Red Fern Grows	Wilson Rawls
A Light in the Attic	Shel Silverstein
Where the Sidewalk Ends	Shel Silverstein
Because of Winn Dixie	Kate DiCamillo
Shiloh	Phyllis Reynolds Naylor
The Best Christmas Pageant Ever	Barbara Robinson

At the conclusion of each book I hung out our sign: **The Absence of Noise is not the Presence of Learning**. The children hurriedly placed their desks in cooperative learning groups as I whispered a quick prayer, and a poem was born! The children volunteered the important facts in each book and I wrote them on the board. I assigned each group with a set of information and they were to create a part of our class poem. I've included a portion of one such poem my class wrote after finishing *Sarah, Plain and Tall*. This book was such a timely book to read to my children. Most of my students were from homes that had lost a parent in their lives through death, imprisonment or divorce. This story let the children see that a family can welcome a new person into their lives that would love and care for them. And that to love this new family member didn't erase the memory of a loved one that had left them. One year I had eight children with a father in prison. Many years the majority of my students were from homes that included stepmothers or stepfathers and the story in this book showed the children how to embrace this new family member.

A Mother and a Friend

By LaTasia Dozier McCann, Jerrell Gandy, Micheal Walley,
Garrett Reynolds, Holly Bedwell Slay, Victoria Boyles Anglin,
DeAlex Paicely, Derek Thornton, Benjamin McIlwain,
Rachael Clark Albury and Megan Shirley Cooley

(1st 4 lines and last 4 lines)

Jacob's wife died so he was sad.

Sarah came from Maine, now he's glad.

Anna wanted a mother more than anything,

She missed the songs her family used to sing.

Jacob and Sarah became man and wife,

They stayed together the rest of their life.

They both started their lives over again.

Now the children have a mother and a friend!

Quite often I would read poetry to my students. Shell Silverstein's books and Dr. Seuss's books were our third grade favorites. Silverstein's "Sarah Cynthia Sylvia Stout Would Not Take the Garbage Out" and "NO Difference" were two of their favorites and often requested! Dr. Seuss Day was a really big deal at our school. The children wore pajamas, brought pillows and blankets and read books all day. Desks were pushed against the walls to make room for a giant pillow party. We, as teachers, had to include educational objectives so we made trail mix using math, a scavenger hunt, writing poetry, spelling games and reading time. I had to have some structure to keep my sanity so I mapped out the day and the kids just thought it was a fun day. The cafeteria got into the fun with serving green eggs and our principal, dressed as The Cat in the Hat, visited each classroom along with Thing 1 and Thing 2. They would barge in, amid the laughter, and try to trash the room. They turned over the desks, threw books and papers onto the floor and entertained each child. At the conclusion of the day, as the blankets were refolded and the pillows and books stuffed into backpacks, missing shoes located and cups of spilled trail mix were swept into piles and discarded, our poetry time began. This is one of the acrostic poems that some of my students composed after a day of fun.

Dr. Fun

By LaTasia Dozier McCann, Jerrell Gandy, Micheal Walley, Garrett Reynolds, Holly Bedwell Slay, Victoria Boyles Anglin, DeAlex Paicely, Derek Thornton, Benjamin McIlwain, Rachael Clark Albury and Megan Shirley Cooley

(1st 4 lines and last 3 lines)
Dr. Fun imagined amazing features,
Really weird and wacky creatures,
Silly stories read by teachers.
Every line had to rhyme,
Unusual characters every time.
Strange aliens and a bad feline creeper,
Sleepy heros and a bossy earth keeper.

I always had a Christmas tree in my classroom and I usually did the decorating after school during the first week of December. As a seasoned teacher, I knew when that tree went up, I better be on my best game! Excitement permeated the classroom! If I could just steer this excitement into learning activities, I would be successful for one more December. This year I let the children decorate the tree which was extra noisy, but fun! A dear parent brought our class a real cedar tree with the roots still attached in a giant bucket! Can you imagine my surprise when this huge lumberjack man lugged this huge, real tree into our classroom? I learned to get more details about gifts, but this tree was the best gift ever! The children had too much fun decorating this giant tree! After this Christmas I welcomed the noise as I let the children decorate our classroom tree and each group of children would write a poem. I've included a portion of one of those poems below.

Christmas Tree Fun

By LaTasia Dozier McCann, Jerrell Gandy, Micheal Walley,
Garrett Reynolds, Holly Bedwell Slay, Victoria Boyles Anglin,
DeAlex Paicely, Derek Thornton, Benjamin McIlwain,
Rachael Clark Albury and Megan Shirley Cooley

(1st 4 lines and last 4 lines)

Decorating a tree is fun!

We will work until it's done.

First, we will put on the lights.

They will make the tree really bright.

Finally, we put on the Christmas star.

Like the one the shepherds saw a far.

Put it by the window for all to see.

A white Christmas, we hope it will be!

We later planted this giant tree out by the cafeteria. I'm sure our custodian thanks us every time he has to mow around the only tree in the yard!

Since I was a cancer survivor, I gladly headed-up our Relay For Life Team at our school. One year I confiscated, without permission, my husband's prized deer head. I attached this deer head to my son's red wagon. I took it to school and used it as one of our fund-raisers for the American Cancer Society. It was a tremendous hit with the children. It cost one dollar to take it to a classroom and then that classroom had to pay one dollar to send it on to another classroom. That secretly appropriated deer-head attached to the red wagon made the rounds of every classroom and several times to the principal's office. I had some explaining to do when my husband noticed the empty space above his chair, but it was so worth the hot water! The children loved it, but I found another way to raise money the next year!

Every year our school had a huge Constitution Day Program. The Daughters of the American Revolution, all local officials, and all parents and grandparents were invited to attend. Classes performed skits, songs, or impersonations of famous Americans. Each grade level performed a song usually with props. The children all had matching shirts and held small flags. We practiced the songs till they were perfectly memorized. The program lasted about an hour and we all whispered a prayer for no rain and no bees or wasps! These programs were the highlight of our principals' year! Right up there with Kindergarten Graduation. In honor of this special day, some of my children wrote a poem celebrating this most important document. I have included a portion of this poem.

The Constitution

By LaTasia Dozier McCann, Jerrell Gandy, Micheal Walley,
Garrett Reynolds, Holly Bedwell Slay, Victoria Boyles Anglin,
DeAlex Paicely, Derek Thornton, Benjamin McIlwain,
Rachael Clark Albury and Megan Shirley Cooley

(1st 4 lines and last 4 lines)
Fifty-five delegates from thirteen states,
Made July 2, 1787, an important date.
The dedicated delegates had divided debates,
While God slowly opened freedom's gates.

In 1787 the Constitution was done,
And joy spread over the land for everyone.
In all fifty states in the U.S.A.
The Constitution is honored to this very day.

The Gifted Teacher requested that it be read aloud at the conclusion of the program that year. It was read at every Constitution Day program till I retired. What an honor for me and especially for my students that year!

THE FRUIT OF PATIENCE

Wherefore seeing we also are compassed about with so great a cloud of witnesses, let us lay aside every weight, and the sin which doth so easily beset us, and let us run with patience the race that is set before us. Hebrews 12:1

One of the most difficult goals to achieve in third grade is the memorization of multiplication facts. I was surprised at the differences in rates of memorization between the academically challenged students and the gifted ones. Every year this was true! The children that normally learned and retained the skills at a slower rate actually mastered the multiplication facts first. This puzzled me! I did some digging and learned that the part of the brain that supported memorization was used more often by the less academically able children than by the gifted children. Gifted children were always able to figure out the answer without using memorization. So I began to search for ways to encourage the gifted to use memorization throughout the day. I had always loved poetry and knew this genre appealed to most children. I knew that memorization of poetry exercised the part of the brain that was also responsible for math facts. My class memorized a poem each month. We would practice the poem while lining up for recess, lunch, music or P.E. or while moving desks for cooperative learning and other times that the children were moving and a cover for the resulting noise was needed. Maybe I needed the distraction to cover the noise, but either way, it worked. Children are going to talk during these times, so I supplied them with a constructive activity. Each student had to be in place by the end of the reciting of the poem. I was even surprised at how well it worked! The children loved reciting the poems and were so happy to share their treasures with all that came by our classroom. I will admit that I was so very proud of them and a bit surprised that third graders could commit so many poems to memory during the year. I would post the monthly poem in several places around our classroom. By the end of the month, the children didn't need to glance at the poems, they were written on their hearts. These are a few of my favorites that would be great for third or fourth graders to memorize. But always choose poetry that speaks to your heart and the heart of your children when making your choice.

I Found A Friend	Author Unknown
September	Rachel Field
Columbus	Author Unknown
I'm A Little Indian	Author Unknown
What Can I Give Him	Christina Rossetti
I'd Like To Be A Lighthouse	Rachel Lyman Field
A Wish For February	Donovan Marshall
An Irish Blessing	Unknown (Attributed to Saint Patrick)
The Reader's Oath	Debra Angstead

By the end of the school year, my class could recite nine poems from memory at one time. This was another wonderful surprise for me and the many visitors that frequented our room. And as a result, the gifted children used memorization to pass the timed multiplication tests. The goal was one hundred problems in three minutes. The children had to score 95% on three multiplication tests on each set to pass to the next set. The students progressed at their own rate. By the end of the year the majority of the class could score 95% or above on one hundred mixed multiplication facts all the way to the twelves! I realized quickly that reciting poetry was the best noise ever and paid amazing dividends!

Our third grade social studies textbook inspired many poems about our government and our country. My class wrote some to remember important facts, some to review for tests instead of study sheets and some just for fun! My class wrote "I'm An American" after we had finished a unit in our textbook describing our flag and famous landmarks. We brainstormed the important details from this unit and I wrote them on the board, I placed our special sign on the outside of our classroom door, whispered a prayer and the children recited a poem as they hurriedly placed their desks into cooperative learning groups of four. We reviewed the guidelines and individual responsibilities for working in groups. I gave each group a sheet of paper and each student a different colored marker so I could be sure each child was participating. The poem that emerged was so meaningful! These thoughtful third graders had captured the essence of being an American. Below you will find a portion of our patriotic poem.

I'm An American

By LaTasia Dozier McCann, Jerrell Gandy, Micheal Walley,
Garrett Reynolds, Holly Bedwell Slay, Victoria Boyles Anglin,
DeAlex Paicely, Derek Thornton, Benjamin McIlwain,
Rachael Clark Albury and Megan Shirley Cooley

(1st 6 lines)

I'm an American,

And I'm blessed as can be,

To live in America,

The land of the free,

Of the soldiers that fought,

To protect our tranquility!

Later that week our local newspaper editor approached our principal about an article for his newspaper. She sent him to our classroom and we shared this poem with him. The children were elated to become published authors in the next edition of our county newspaper!

At the conclusion of our unit on the seven continents, our class created a class poem to use as a review for the upcoming quiz. I hung our sign on the classroom door signaling a noisy time endorsed by the teacher and whispered a quick prayer. With this poem we stayed in groups of two or four and was it ever noisy, but very productive! Again the children brainstormed to create a list of important information on the seven continents. I had already compiled a list and the children hit every single detail! As you can read in the portion of the resulting poem, the children were becoming proficient with including details and using poetry to broaden their world.

Our World

By LaTasia Dozier McCann, Jerrell Gandy, Micheal Walley,
Garrett Reynolds, Holly Bedwell Slay, Victoria Boyles Anglin,
DeAlex Paicely, Derek Thornton, Benjamin McIlwain,
Rachael Clark Albury and Megan Shirley Cooley

(1st 8 lines)
Lands and water, water and lands,
God holds it all in His hands.
What do you see in the Western Hemisphere?
North America, South America: It's very clear!
North America has deserts,
forests and grassland.
And 429 million people: Wow, that's grand!
The United States, Canada,
Mexico and Greenland,
On this vast continent, we proudly stand.

Through the years I have saved some of the poems that my students have written. Sharing a few with you would be my joy! These two poems, about their principals, were written in cooperative groups. The inspiration for both these poems came from the poem, "Who" written by Shel Silverstein in his book, *Where the Sidewalk Ends*. Mrs. Britton was our lead principal and always searched for ways to make learning fun for the children. She visited our classroom often and encouraged each child to do his best. I always sent a copy of our edited poems to her and she would write encouraging notes back to our class. We treasured these notes! I have included a portion of this poem below.

Mrs. Britton

By LaTasia Dozier McCann, Jerrell Gandy, Micheal Walley,
Garrett Reynolds, Holly Bedwell Slay, Victoria Boyles Anglin,
DeAlex Paicely, Derek Thornton, Benjamin McIlwain,
Rachael Clark Albury and Megan Shirley Cooley

(1ˢᵗ 4 lines and last 3 lines)
She's Intelligent, awesome and graceful.
She's a Christian, magnificent and successful.

She brought Accelerated Reading to our school.
We earn points to go somewhere cool.

In this school you are a very special part.
You have made us truly smart.
Thank you from the bottom of our heart!

Dr. Herring was the gifted teacher before she became our third and fourth grade principal. Many of my students had been in her gifted class before she became a principal and they remembered her talking of her quest to get her doctor's degree. Below you will find a portion of this poem.

Dr. Herring

By Judy Roberts, Madison Ashley and Reid Cooley

(1st 4 lines and last 3 lines)
She's a teacher, a role model,
and now a principal.
She's friendly, nice and extremely sensible.
I love her hugs, kisses, and smiles,
With our education she'll go many miles.

Congratulations, a hug and a kiss.
Thank you for your loyalness.
With you W.E.S. is heavenly bliss!

My favorite book to use in my poetry lessons was *Favorite Poetry Lessons* by Paul B. Janeczko.

His "How To" lessons were perfect for my third grade class. Below you will find several of my favorites born from his inspiration. Each poem was placed in a clear plastic bag and the bags were stapled together for a class book. These plastic books were always a favorite in our class library!

Without

By Micheal Walley, Benjamin McIlwain
and Garrett Reynolds

(1st 4 lines and last 4 lines)
School without teachers
Football without bleachers
A girl without hair
Facts of Life without Blair

A spring without a fling
A finger without a ring
Homer Simpson without fat
A cat without a rat

Useless Things

By Holly Bedwell Slay, Victoria Boyles
Anglin and Megan Shirley

A clock without a tock
A key without a lock
Ground without rocks
Feet without socks
A moon without light
A sky that isn't bright

The assignment for the next poems was to choose a topic, brainstorm characteristics of the topic and write a poem.

As I reread each of these poems, I am in awe of the creativity of each child!

Lunch

By Madison Ashley and Reid Cooley

I had to stand in line for lunch one day,
Till the teacher said I had to pay.
I told her I left my money on the bus,
But she didn't believe me and then she fussed!
Finally, my friend gave me some money.

And I told her she was as sweet as honey!
What am I suppose to do?
Because that was all my money.
But I don't care because she's my friend.
And now I am telling you, this is the end!

Blue

Brittany Harrison

It is dark.
It can mark.
Blue
I like that color.
It is cool.
It can move.
Blue
I like that color.
It is light.
It is bright.
Blue
I like that color.
It is smooth.
It is cool.
Blue
I like that color.

Charsie

By Lexi Bowen

She has a cat.
It is fat.
Charsie
I like that girl
She likes to play with toys.
She loves all the boys.
Charsie
I like that girl.
She loves to talk.
But not to walk.
Charsie
I like that girl.
Charsie is my friend.
And she is with me to the end.
Charsie
I like that girl.

Ghouls

By Brianna Mills Smith

They swim in a pool.
They like to drool.
Ghouls
They go to school.
They don't follow the rules.
Ghouls
They catch the flu.
They wear only one shoe.
Ghouls
They don't have looks.
They can't read books.
Ghouls

When I Am Alone

By Lexi Bowen and Charsie Duvall

I like to read books,
When my mother cooks.
I like to swim,
While she goes to the gym.
I like to ride my bike,

With my friend Mike.
I like to watch TV,
But my mom won't let me be.
She likes to play with her cat.
It is fat.
She likes to play soccer,
While I put things in my locker.
We like to go to the mall,
Especially in the fall.
We like to eat our snacks,
That are in our backpacks.
We like to play in the playhouse,
Unless we see a mouse.
We like to talk on the phone,
When my mother is gone.
We are best friends,
And that is the end!

These next poems were the result of determining the steps that go into doing your best in school and in life. Our reading skill for this activity was cause and effect. I whispered a silent, "Thank You," as I read the references to spiritual experiences that always make their way into the children's compositions.

My Best

By LaTasia Dozier McCann, Jerrell Gandy, Micheal Walley,
Garrett Reynolds, Holly Bedwell Slay, Victoria Boyles Anglin,
DeAlex Paicely, Derek Thornton, Benjamin McIlwain,
Rachael Clark Albury and Megan Shirley Cooley

(1st 4 lines and last 4 lines)
Study hard, try your best,
You will make 100 on a test.
Practice piano, do your best,
After the recital, you can rest.

Read a lot of books, get a star,
You might even win a car!
Read the Bible, be a Christian,
You will learn how to listen.

Reach For The Stars

By LaTasia Dozier McCann, Jerrell Gandy, Micheal Walley,
Garrett Reynolds, Holly Bedwell Slay, Victoria Boyles Anglin,
DeAlex Paicely, Derek Thornton, Benjamin McIlwain,
Rachael Clark Albury and Megan Shirley Cooley

(1st 4 lines and last 4 lines)
Study hard and do your best,
Make a 100 on your test.
Practice gymnastics as a mission,

Do well in your competition.
Go to church and learn new songs,
Sing well on choir day morns.
Read lots of books in your own space,
Go to McDonald's Play Place!

Reading the poetry of my students was like
Christmas morning! Their poetry was the best
gift ever to the heart of this thankful teacher.
Each poem was so worth the noise and will always
be treasured by me!

5

THE FRUIT OF FAITH

And we know that all things work together for good to them that love God, to them who are the called according to his purpose. Romans 8:28

God sends me many children each year and I have come to learn that all children are gifted! God gives each child a gift and I saw so many different gifts through the years. Of course children are gifted in numerous academic areas, but the giftedness that I want to relate is a giftedness of the heart and of faith. As I think about the gift of kindness, I think of a special young man that surprised the new student and us with a huge welcome sign. The sweet girl had never attended school and was way behind in her studies. I explained this to the children and asked them to be patient with her. She lacked social skills as well as academic skills. With the help of each child in our classroom, we encouraged her to learn. She bloomed! She was behind two grade levels in all subject areas. Within nine weeks she had caught up with the class. The smile on her face as she learned was priceless and the lesson learned by my class that year was invaluable. With acceptance and love my whole class became her family. Makes my heart smile to remember how we all grew in kindness and patience that year. And it all began with a young man's gift of a kind heart and a big sign!

The gift of love certainly applied to a particular young man in my class one year. He was struggling in reading and the main problem was that he wasn't doing homework or completing the assignments in oral reading at home. After a couple of weeks, I contacted our counselor and she set up a meeting with his mother. He wasn't a discipline problem at all, sometimes too quiet for a third grader. Well, the principal, the counselor, his mom and I all met one morning. Boy, were my eyes opened! He was the oldest of five children. His mother was a "lady of the night" and there was no father in the picture for any of the children. This precious child protected and cared for his four siblings all night and was even responsible for preparing meals. I remembered he would tell me that he could cook macaroni and cheese and other simple dishes. I never dreamed that he was carrying this load of responsibility! I still tear-up when I think of this child gifted with so much love for his little family. I thank God that my eyes were opened! I found ways during school to help him with his homework and to practice oral reading with a partner. This tiny voice reading was the sweetest noise to this teacher's heart. It's hard to comprehend that an eight year old was the adult in the family. I watched this young man as he progressed through the grades at our school. This gift of love for his family blossomed into integrity, confidence and maturity. There's one thing that I'm sure of: if he is a daddy, he's the best daddy in the whole world!

Some children had the gift of energy! I tried to view this gift as an asset. A young man one particular year was determined to stay at my desk and talk or visit with his neighbor. I learned that if I would appeal to his sense of empathy, we would survive his "noise". I'd tell him that another student needed his help and that for the next fifteen minutes he could help this child and the conversation would be fine. I knew that when children worked as a team, they both learned from each other. He loved working with other children and helping them solve each problem. He is a lawyer today!

Some children had the gift of organization. I only had to look at their locker or school box to see this awesome gift. I learned that the reminders of," It's lunchtime or recess or PE," were noises that I should be grateful for! I was always blessed with a precious child each year that helped me organize our time. One such little girl one year kept my desk nice and neat all year. She was a treasure and she is a teacher today. I can just see her teacher's desk! Every piece of paper is filed, there is a tray for homework and classwork and there are twenty sharpened pencils in a can on her desk. She knows exactly where her grade book is in case of a fire drill. How do I know this? She always remembered to get that gradebook as I led our class out of the room.

Some children had the gift of resilience. These children always tugged at my heart as they rose above their circumstances to succeed in school. One year I had eight students in my classroom with a parent in prison. One little girl was being held by her mother when her father shot and killed this precious child's mother. I prayed a lot that year! Several of these children were being raised by grandmothers or even great-grandmothers. These precious ladies will always be so special to me. The life-line that they provided for these little ones, with few resources, will always be appreciated by me and by their grandchild.

Some children had the gift of compassion. Just let a box of sixty-four crayons hit the floor and half the class would rush to help. Those sixty-four crayons would be picked up in one minute flat. This was a noise that always made me stop and whisper a thank you to the One above.

Some children had the gift of observation. One such young man would watch me every time I went to one of the computers in the classroom and logged in. He figured out all my pass codes and passwords. I noticed that the screen was frequently changed and I couldn't figure out what was happening. My whole class figured out what was going on before I even had a clue! We all shared a loud and noisy laugh the day I finally realized who the culprit was. I came to rely on his expertise with technology and he often rescued this teacher from a complete technology disaster! He is a computer whiz today and I'm sure he is still changing the screens of unsuspecting victims!

When I think of the gift of loving all things great and small, I think of one young giant that only wanted to be a farmer. If he drew a picture, it was a cow. If he wrote an essay, it always included a tractor and a barn. He had the sweetest spirit and was so gentle even though he was a head taller than anyone in our class. I could hear those boots he always wore coming down our hallway and knew that a future farmer was in our midst. And today he spends his days caring for the most gentle of God's creatures. God reveals in the hearts of some third graders their life work and begins to mold their hearts to love what God loves. It was truly a joy to teach this young man and to view from afar his dreams coming true.

When I think about the gift of courage, the memory of one young boy floods my mind. He was involved in an accident during a football game that resulted in surgery to set his broken upper leg. I still remember the day he came back to school with an exposed metal frame and in a wheel chair. My mind exploded with so many thoughts like how in the world would I keep him safe and free from germs. But the children in our classroom certainly rose to the occasion with their noisy volunteers of assistance and the good Lord calmed my fears! The boys took turns pushing his wheel chair around the campus. I'm sure there were times that this sweet child was in pain, uncomfortable or embarrassed, but he NEVER complained. We were all so happy for him on the day that the doctors pronounced him healed and removed the exposed metal frame! But our joy was soon replaced with the sad fact that his limb wasn't healed. This brave child had to endure another surgery to have the exposed metal brace replaced. Every child in our classroom was moved to tears as well as this brokenhearted teacher. Life just isn't fair sometimes! Well, Superchild returned to school with the metal brace and in a wheelchair for the second time that year. And again he NEVER complained! It's a lot to ask a third-grade child to form lasting character and a strong faith, but he rose to the occasion! He is currently working on a master's degree in our local college, but I know his skills to cope with life began in third grade as God gifted this sweet boy with a courageous faith that is still so strong today.

I have taught many children through the years that I was so honored to catch a glimpse of their future work. I fondly remember a beautiful young lady that aspired to become a writer and was always creating stories that literally danced off the pages of her tablet. I know she has published one book and hopefully more will be added through the years. I once taught a young man that read the encyclopedias in his free time and is now a world traveler and very well educated. He beat out a path around the world and gifted me with the New Zealand coin that he kept in his pocket during his travels. What a beautiful gift and a thoughtful young man. Every time he left his desk to retrieve the next volume, I would think, "What a great man he will be. God is preparing him for awesome things." What a joy it has become to view from afar his travels and accomplishments!

I came to realize that these gifts were sometimes clothed in a little noise. I had to look past the disruption to see a child's treasured gift. What a joy when I would see these gifts working their magic! Our whole class was blessed and my faith in God's purpose for me became crystal clear.

6

THE FRUIT OF SELF-CONTROL

> A word fitly spoken is like apples of gold in pictures of silver.
> Proverbs 25:11

Some classroom noise I will never understand. The Holy Spirit certainly gifted me with the fruit of self-control throughout my teaching career! I am truly amazed that unwise and hurtful words didn't just tumble out of my mouth like rocks down a steep mountain on some of these occasions. I'm so thankful that God reminded me that children have tender hearts and it was my responsibility to protect these sweetest of hearts.

One Christmas the students drew names to purchase gifts. Most classes did this and I had never had a problem. Of course I had purchased several extra boy and extra girl gifts just in case. I was truly surprised when one little girl cried that morning because her gift was a pearl necklace and she wanted a toy. I gave her one of the gifts that I had brought and told her that her gift came in two packages. She was happy, but that was the last year we drew names! The next year each parent sent a gift for their own child. Problem solved!

I'm still puzzled by this incident! The lunch lady brought it to my attention that one of my students hid ice cream as she went through the lunch line. Ice cream was not included in the meal, so the children had to pay extra. Now this little girl was dressed like a princess every day. She had anything a little girl could possibly want or need. Well, I spoke with her father and related the incident. He didn't seem surprised at all. He handed me a ten dollar bill and asked if I would pay for the ice cream and give her the change for the concession stand. I'm sure I just stood there with my mouth wide open! Give her the change? I promptly paid for the stolen treat and placed the nine dollars in an envelope and returned it to him the next day. I never mentioned the incident to the child, but she never took anything else that year that didn't belong to her. Sometimes silence speaks that loudest language of all!

✠ Even a child is known by his do-
ings, whether his work be pure,
and whether it be right. Proverbs 20:11

Another day an irate mother showed up at my classroom door. This was so against the rules. She was to go by the office, get a pass and the secretary would buzz me over the intercom of the visitor. She demanded to know why I had paddled her child. The noise was so loud from her complaints that I couldn't think. I asked the child in question to come speak with his mother and with me. He admitted that he had told his mom a big fib! No apology from mom or the child. Her next words were that the homework the night before was too hard. I'm still confused over that one! The apple never falls far from the tree! This is my first thought when a child acts just like a parent.

As many teachers from small towns can relate, I've had more teacher conferences at stores than I have ever had at school. One Sunday afternoon my mother needed to buy fabric and thread. She loved to quilt! I normally never shop on Saturday or Sunday afternoons but I needed to go as well. A parent of one of my precious students was bored with his wife's shopping and spied my mother and me in the fabric department. I'm so thankful that the Holy Spirit filled my heart with self-control that Sunday afternoon as I took the time to ignore my list and listen to the love this parent had for his child. I learned a very valuable lesson that Sunday afternoon; being too busy will rob me of the most precious of blessings! I still venture into these stores and enjoy visiting with busy parents and children that I have taught. The Lord has blessed me over the years with these helpful and valuable conversations that have touched this teacher's heart.

As I'm sure you have noticed, these noisy times were few and far between and have helped me learn valuable lessons. The happy times always outweigh the stressful times when I remember how blessed I was when God made me a teacher and gave me a teacher's heart.

> Trust in the Lord with all thine heart; and lean not unto thine own understanding. Proverbs 3:5

7

THE FRUIT OF GOODNESS, KINDNESS AND GENTLENESS

 Be Still, and Know that I am God: I
will be exalted among the heathen, I
will be exalted in the earth. Psalm 46:10

I serve on Wednesday nights in a children's program at my church we call Kids' Café. This program was begun by a lady and her mother to meet
the spiritual needs of little girls. This program has
grown from four or five little girls to an attendance
of fifty to sixty and sometimes seventy boys and
girls from 4 years old to youth age. God called adults
to serve in Kids' Café that really love children and

want these children to become Christians. God has truly blessed these children and adults and I am so thankful to be a small part of showing these children the love of Jesus. The joy outweighs the challenges, but there are challenges for this retired school teacher. Anyone can tell you that I am not a fan of noisy, loud and moving children during mealtime. My siblings or I weren't allowed to talk during mealtimes and I guess this practice has stuck with me. Sometimes it's so noisy during the meal portion of Kids' Café that I slip outside to gather my thoughts before my class begins. But I began to actually see what a wonderful miracle was happening in the midst of all that noise. The little girls were laughing, sharing food and sometimes playing tag because they had grown to love each other during their time at Kids' Café. The little boys were sharing funny stories and telling about their last time at bat or their last free throw that produced "nothing but net"! These young boys were learning to love each other, as well. The older boys were sharing something funny on their phones, getting another plate of food, thanking the ladies for the delicious food and learning to love and appreciate each other. The older girls, that always sit at the corner table, were discussing school, boys, things that break their hearts and learning to love each other. The adults were finally having time to visit and share funny pictures on their phones of their children and learning to love and depend on each other. The adults that serve during Kids' Café on Wednesday night at our church are all different ages, employed in different professions or retired and all join to learn to serve and to love the children that the Good Lord sends on Wednesday night. I came to see that the noise had a mission: the joy of souls and spirits that meet and learn to love each other. Even though these children are from very different backgrounds, different schools and different races, they meet at Kids' Café on level ground at the feet of our Savior. Each adult that serves in this awesome ministry completely relies on God's provision, protection and providing the message for each lesson. In the midst of this noisy crew, I am realizing that love is surrounding me. This makes my heart smile! I'm so thankful for this poem that God laid on my heart one morning during my devotion time.

You and I

By Judy Roberts

With children I must love
outside my comfort zone.
With God's help, I'll speak
with my most loving tone.
Being a little uncomfortable
might be God's will.
Listen to God and be perfectly still.
He has a mission for all of us to do.
Will I be Your Heart to love
the children for You?

We usually have to run two van loads to pick up the children, but those of us without children at home, volunteer to take a family of children home. I was taking a family of sweet children home one night and one of the boys asked me to turn up the radio. It was already so noisy with five extra children! But I turned up the volume and I'm so glad that I did! That sweet boy shouted, "I know that song! My grandma sings it all the time. She's a Christian." Out of the mouth of babes! We should make sure our grandchildren know! I'm so thankful for this child's grandmother and I'm so thankful that I saw a glimpse of Heaven on Earth that night. Even in the midst of the noise, I learned that children are so perceptive, marvelously made and have a heart that recognizes Jesus!

In August, 2019, the children of Kids' Café packed Goodie Bags for the teachers and staff at our local elementary school. I'm so glad that one of our sweet ladies with two grandchildren in our program wanted to create a service project for the children and youth. The children were excited to be a part of recognizing their new teacher for the year with a gift. Was it ever noisy but our goal was met! We packed over 100 bags! The children that attended a different school were given bags to give to their teachers. This is the poem that we attached to each bag.

Appreciation

By Judy Roberts

Love and goodies in a
simple brown bag.
Packed by Kids' Café and
sealed with this tag.
Prayed over with you in our hearts.
A little appreciation before
the school year starts!

Because of Covid19 we have not been able to have Kids' Café since March of 2020. At the suggestion of a sweet lady, I started writing letters each week to my little girls' class. Each Monday as I walk, God lays on my heart the verse and the story from the Bible verse to include in the letter. I'm so thankful for this opportunity God has given to me and the reminder that even in the midst of a pandemic, He is still on His throne! Well, it's November and God's Holy Spirit is still laying the stories and verses on my heart. I don't know why we Christians worry; God always has a plan!

> But the Comforter, which is the Holy Ghost, whom the Father will send in my name, He shall teach you all things, and bring all things to your remembrance, whatsoever I have said unto you. John 14:26

THE FRUIT OF PEACE

For I know the thoughts that I think toward you, saith the Lord, thoughts of peace, and not of evil, to give you an expected end. Jeremiah 29:11

I was so blessed to obtain a college degree in education. My father passed when I was only fourteen and my mother had to go to work to feed my brother and me. She only had a ninth grade education and had never worked outside the home. When I think of my mama, I know that God gave me the best! Preparation for the Lord's Day began on Saturday in our home when I was a child. Everyone's hair was washed and curled, Sunday clothes were ironed and Sunday School Lessons were studied. Because my daddy worked away from home in the oilfield and we only had one car, we had to walk to church many Sundays but someone always graciously took us home. My mama was a strong prayer warrior. She had survived almost any tragedy possible: the loss of a child in a fire, the loss of her husband with small children to raise and cancer. My mama was determined that I would earn a college degree. She and I watched the sunrise for nearly two years as she waited with me to catch the bus to Jones Junior College. God provided and I received two scholarships which paid for my junior college education. Later, I worked as a teacher's assistant and attended night school. My husband, Tommy, wanted me to continue my education as much as Mama did and provided the resources to complete my degree. I graduated with a degree in Elementary Education and was hired as a first grade teacher for the second semester at the same school where I worked as an assistant. Back in those days, if a teacher became pregnant in the first semester, she had to stay home the second semester. I know, it makes no sense! I felt so sad for the teacher, but those were the rules. I had thirty first grade students with no assistant. I managed four reading groups each morning and the children were so very well behaved. That first semester teacher had trained her children well and I was so thankful! God opened every door for me to become a teacher and I should have had more faith in His Plan when I got sick!

> Yea, though I walk through the
> valley of the shadow of death, I
> will fear no evil: for thou art with me;
> thy rod and thy staff they comfort me.
> Psalm 23:4

During the spring of one school year, I kept having a sore throat. After several trips to several different doctors, I was diagnosed with non-Hodgkins Lymphoma in my right tonsil. Throat cancer and I needed my voice to teach! The day before I went for my first chemo, I dropped by the school to let my class know why I was absent, and that I would be back soon, even though I didn't get to come back that year. That was the hardest day ever! Harder than letting my whole class miss the bus on the first day of school, harder than the day one of my students climbed out the bathroom window and walked home, and almost harder than sitting with one of my little girls as she said goodbye to her mother. Our poor coach was in the hallway as I exited my classroom. I cried and boo-hooed all over him! That was a noisy and difficult season, but I have never felt closer to God. My last radiation treatment was on a Thursday and the children's first day was Friday. I had used all my sick days the previous year and I thought I had to return for my insurance. My sweet principal stayed in contact with me throughout that summer of treatments and secured a retired teacher to help me during those first few weeks. Just like an unruly child, God let me have my way to return too soon and I ended up back in the hospital. I'm sure that if I had listened to God, He would have made an easier way. This "valley of the shadow of death" is a walk that I will always remember: the endless doctor visits, surgery, tests, nights in the hospital and missing my family. As I look at this season through my rear-view mirror, God's love and protection sustained me as He still does today. God is always with us when we need Him the most, and He is most assuredly there to comfort and provide peace in the midst of the noise.

For His anger endureth but a moment; in his favor is life: weeping may endure for a night, but joy cometh in the morning. Psalm 30:5

I've often thought about why God allowed me to have cancer. I still don't have that answer, but I can finally say, "Thank you, Lord." Thank You for seeing me through that dark and lonely time. I call it my time in the desert. God was only a whisper away and He cared, comforted and protected me. I'm so thankful He sent the BEST principal, Mary Annie Ezell, to take care of my little ones at school. God even made a way for my husband to come home to take care of me. Tommy resigned a very lucrative position in Houston and started a small pump company. Tommy worked hard and God blessed his efforts. Girls, when you are looking for a husband, pick one that loves God and loves his mama. The way he loves his mama is the way he will love his wife! Our oldest son was in college at MS State University and our youngest son was attending Wayne County High School. I'm so thankful to God for caring for my family when I couldn't. My husband, my family, my church family, my school family and my best friend truly supported me! I was never alone, God was there every step of the way and quieted the noise in my troubled heart.

My Life

By Judy Roberts

A beautiful home, a yard full of flowers,
Thank You for making it all ours.
We know all good things come from You,
Family, church and friendships, too!
Give me a thankful and generous heart.
Help me to serve, to do my part.
Make me useful in Your great plan,
Help me to complete this race, we can!
One day it's to Heaven, I'm bound,
According to Your Word, I've always found,
Jesus is the only way, it's printed there,
For your soul, He will always care,
Give your heart to the lover of your soul,
In life, this should be our only goal.

9

IN CLOSING

✠ Study to show thyself approved
unto God, a workman that need-
eth not to be ashamed, rightly dividing
the word of truth. 2 Timothy 2:15

I try to complete a devotion each morning and write in my journal. Journaling has been a passion in my life forever. I have filled many, many different journals with prayers, hopes, dreams and found peace for my soul. I have a favorite place that I like to pray and when life takes an unexpected turn or a burden is too heavy to carry alone, I always return to this place and talk to God. He always listens! I have even on occasion pleaded with Him to help me find things that I have put away for safe keeping. My husband and I have been married for almost fifty years and through these years I have been gifted with three sets of wedding rings. I know, three sets of rings makes no sense, but now I have three granddaughters and each one will have a set! God knew what I would need even when I didn't! Anyway, I put two sets up for safekeeping and promptly forgot where I placed them. After about four years of looking, I finally got onto my knees in my favorite place and prayed. About two minutes later, I came across my rings! God is so good to His children even the forgetful ones! This poem came about one morning as I was writing in my journal. I never know when God will gift me with a poem, but it is always a precious treasure.

Peace

By Judy Roberts

I'm hiding behind Your amazing grace,
Peaceful and happy; It's the best place!
Thank you for my peaceful abode,
Away from Life's impossible load.
A place of rest, to be with You,
Opening my eyes to Your promises, so true.
Helping me remember to run here each day,
To relieve my fears and drive my worries away,
To enjoy and love each beautiful day!
Are you looking for peace amid life's daily strife?
Are you struggling to be a Christian wife?
Jesus is waiting with your wonderful life.
So spend time with Him each and every day,
And read the Bible, It points the way!

As I walk and ponder the future of my grand-children, I can sometimes catch a glimpse of the gifts that God has placed into their hearts. Claire loves to sing and Anna loves to paint and draw. Their moms have recognized, encouraged and cultivated these talents. Addie is a born leader and always has a group of friends around. Trey loves puppies, playing outside and waffles. I pray every day that God will use their talents and gifts to enrich their lives and the lives of all they en-counter as they dance down the path God has planned for each one of them.

As I walk on other days, my heart and mind are bombarded with the reminders of the many blessings from my Lord. Shouts of "I am so blessed!" ring in my mind and my heart. I have read that true worship is a heart overflowing with thankfulness to God. Today my heart overflows!

> Call unto me and I will answer thee, and shew thee great and mighty things, which thou knowest not. Jeremiah 33:3

I know now why God gifted me with this story and encouraged me to record each part. He knew that I would look back on these days of amazement, joy and peace to carry me through the lonely days ahead. It's been three weeks since my Tommy, my love, passed so peacefully from this life to his Heavenly home with Jesus. As we stood side by side, held hands and Tommy thanked God for a good day, neither of us knew that in one hour his good day would become a great day! The glorious day he went into the presence of our Jesus. And one great day I'll go to be with my Jesus, too! Until then, I'll continue on this path You have prepared for me and praise You for Your love, joy, peace, faith, patience, goodness, kindness, gentleness and self-control. My heart is still full and my cup continues to run over with God's love and my precious memories.

REFERENCES

Janeczko, Paul. Favorite Poetry Lessons. New York: Scholastic, Inc., 1998.

King James Version Bible. Grand Rapids, Michigan: Zondervan Publishing House, 2000

MacLachlan, Patricia. Sarah, Plain and Tall. New York: Harper & Row, 1985

Seuss, Dr. The Cat In the Hat. New York: Random House, 1957

Seuss, Dr. The Cat In the Hat Comes Back. New York: Random House, 1958

Silverstein, Shel. Where the Sidewalk Ends. New York: Harper & Row, 1974.